MIA BELONGS HERE

Mia Belongs Here is a beautifully illustrated story book introducing five characters: Mia, Ying, Zainab, Dom, and Willow. Each character shows how they know they belong through their different senses, be it hearing dogs charging down the hallway, smelling a sister's incense candles, or tasting fresh tomatoes from the garden.

With its engaging illustrations and narrative, children are encouraged to mindfully think of the sounds, smells, tastes, sights, and sensations that make them feel like they belong, sharing the message that belonging is largely experiential and special to each person.

Belonging is a fundamental building block in the wellbeing of children. In a world of increasing rates of loneliness, disconnection and social isolation, opportunities to encourage a feeling of belonging in children have never been more vital. This story provides a unique opportunity for children to practice mindfulness, to pause and fully engage with the place and moment they're in. By focusing on their senses during the fun, interactive moments, this book promotes a greater sense of belonging in children.

Michael Wagner is the Melbourne-based author of more than 90 books for children including the much-loved, 20-book Maxx Rumble series, the CBCA Honor book *Dirt by Sea* and Notable books *Why I Love Footy*, *Why I Love Summer*, and *Bear Make Den*, and the YABBA, KOALA, and KROC Awards shortlisted So Wrong series. Before becoming an author, Michael worked for ten years as a radio broadcaster with the ABC, wrote and produced award-winning animation for television, and penned everything from advertising copy to songs and comedy.

Kelly-Ann Allen is an Associate Professor and Educational and Developmental Psychologist at Monash University and an Honorary Principal Fellow at the Centre for Wellbeing Science at the University of Melbourne. Kelly-Ann is renowned for her impactful research on belonging, particularly in educational settings, which has earned her recognition as one of Australia's top researchers. Kelly-Ann is dedicated to translating her extensive research into practical applications to benefit educators, students, and broader communities. Her work extends beyond academia, aiming to enhance belonging across populations globally.

Kathryn Kallady is an Educational and Developmental Psychologist. She has worked predominantly with children and their families between the ages of 2–18 years of age. She has extensive experience working with schools in the private and public sectors as well as in public health settings. She has also worked in a private practice confident in neurodevelopmental assessment and therapy. She has worked at Monash University in a supervisory and teaching capacity. Apart from psychology, Kathryn loves illustration and graphic design. She has provided works for academic texts and resources. She is best known for providing the single artwork for Gotye's international hit song, "Somebody that I Used to Know."

Mia Belongs Here

A Story About Family, Home and a Sense of Belonging

Michael Wagner and Kelly-Ann Allen
Illustrated by Kathryn Kallady

Routledge
Taylor & Francis Group

LONDON AND NEW YORK

Designed cover image: Kathryn Kallady

First published 2025
by Routledge
4 Park Square, Milton Park, Abingdon, Oxon OX14 4RN

and by Routledge
605 Third Avenue, New York, NY 10158

Routledge is an imprint of the Taylor & Francis Group, an informa business

British Library Cataloguing-in-Publication Data
A catalogue record for this book is available from the British Library

ISBN: 978-1-032-46576-0 (pbk)
ISBN: 978-1-003-38234-8 (ebk)

This book can also be purchased as part of a set: *Conceptual Playworlds for Belonging* (set),
978-1-032-46583-8

DOI: 10.4324/9781003382348

Typeset in Minion Pro
by Deanta Global Publishing Services, Chennai, India

For Product Safety Concerns and Information please contact our EU representative GPSR@taylorandfrancis.com Taylor & Francis Verlag GmbH, Kaufingerstraße 24, 80331 München, Germany.
Batch No. NP105633

Michael

For Ollie-Sue who belongs right here with us, forever.

Kelly

To every student who enters school in search of belonging—may you find a place where you are seen, valued, and truly loved.

To Florence, Henry, and Georgie—may your school days be filled with learning, laughter, and a lasting sense of belonging.

This is Mia.
These are her ears.

This is Ying.
These are his hands.

This is Zainab.
This is her nose.

This is Dom.
This is his mouth.

And this is Willow.
These are her eyes.

Mia knows she's home when she hears:

Dad making the stove go
click, click, click

the dogs charging down the hallway

whenever someone's at the door …

magpies warbling outside the
open back door

cicadas trilling and buzzing
through the front door

3

the tiny rattle the vent makes when warm air blows through it

and Mia's little brother singing on the other side of the bedroom wall.

These are the *sounds* of home for Mia. And Mia belongs here.

What are the special sounds that feel like home to you? Can you think of five of them?

Ying knows he's home when he feels:

the passing trains making the floor gently rumble

sticky crayons in his fingertips

warm, soapy bath water all around him

the worn-out bit of Panda's tummy

the sheet rubbing up against his chin as he drifts off to sleep

and being hugged by Mummy.

This is what home *feels* like to Ying. And Ying belongs here.

Can you think of five feelings that are special to your home?

Zainab knows she's home when she smells:

Mum's perfume in the hallway

Dad's hair when he's giving her a shoulder-ride

meat cooking on the barbecue

12

incense candles burning in her big sister's room

the white flowers her grandma, Jida, puts in a little vase

and rose-water droplets on her pillowcase.

These are the *smells* of home for Zainab. And Zainab belongs here.

Can you think of five special, lovely smells that make you feel like you're home?

Dom knows he's home when he tastes:

a big, juicy tomato that's still warm from Nonno's garden

ice cold water straight from the fridge

Nonna's bolognese sauce

Mum's salami pizza

Aunty Maria's home-made frozen yoghurt

and minty toothpaste before bedtime.

These are the *tastes* of home for Dom. And Dom belongs here.

Can you think of five delicious flavours that taste like home to you?

Willow knows she's home when she sees:

a jar of Vegemite on the kitchen bench

Mum's muddy boots by the back door

everyone's socks hanging on the line

her dog lying by the fire, asleep

tall trees swaying in the wind outside her window

and lights from the
TV flickering in
the hallway as she's
drifting off the sleep.

This is what home *looks* like to Willow. And Willow belongs here.

Can you think of five sights that make you feel like you're at home?

There are many sights, sounds, smells, tastes, and things you can touch that feel like home.

And every single one of them reminds you that …

you belong here.

ABOUT THIS BOOK

Thank you for taking the time to read our book and for helping the children in your life develop a stronger sense of belonging.

Belonging is often described as a fundamental human need and has been found to be an essential component of wellbeing, physical health, prosocial behaviour, and academic outcomes. It can also buffer the effects of mental illness and can be a protective factor against depression and anxiety.

Belonging is largely experiential and sensory, and can be linked to certain sounds, smells, sights, textures, tastes, and sensations, which are unique and special to each person. This book encourages the reader, through the practice of mindfulness, to pause and fully engage with the place and moment they're in. By focusing on their senses during the fun, interactive moments, the reader's sense of belonging is amplified.

We all need to belong – to family, home, school, nature, the community, and the world. Our hope is that this deceptively simple book promotes a greater sense of belonging in children.